A SNOWY CHRISTMAS STORY

by Santa's Li'l Helpers

"Make Readers Happy."

A Snowy Christmas Story
Hardcover ISBN 978-1-939953-70-4
Paperback ISBN 978-1-939953-66-7
E-Book ISBN 978-1-939953-67-4

Published by Walking Carnival Books
an imprint of Nappaland Communications Inc.
1437 Denver Ave. #193, Loveland, CO 80538
www.WalkingCarnival.com | www.Nappaland.com

Copyright © 2025 Nappaland Communications Inc. All rights reserved. No part of this publication may be reproduced, stored in a retrieval system, or transmitted in any form or by any means without the prior written permission of the publisher.

Public Notice: *A Snowy Christmas Story* is a human-created product. No artificial intelligence (AI) was used to make the text or illustrations. Thank you for supporting creative work by real, actual people.

Editorial: Alec Smart
Cover & Interior Design: WC Creative
Santa's Li'l Helpers: Mike Nappa & Dennis Edwards

Walking Carnival™, and the Walking Carnival colophon are trademarks of Nappaland Communications Inc. All rights reserved.

First Printing

1 2 3 4 5 6 7 • • • 2029 2028 2027 2026 2025

LAST DECEMBER TWENTY-FIVE,
THE SNOW CAME DOWN AT NORTH
POLE DRIVE.

IT COVERED EVERY HOUSE AND TREE,
AND FILLED IN STREETS FROM A TO Z!

i SAW iT WHEN iT SNOWED THAT DAY...

TWO POLAR BEARS CAME OUT TO PLAY!

THEY BUILT ONE SNOWMAN BUT WEREN'T DONE.

THEY BUILT ANOTHER JUST FOR FUN.

A GREAT WHITE TIGER WALKED BY THEN

AND TRAMPLED ON THE BEARS' SNOWMEN!

**NEXT CAME SUE, WITH YULETIDE GLEE.
SHE BROUGHT ALONG A CHRISTMAS TREE!**

THREE WHITE MICE MARCHED ON THE LAWN,

AND SCARED POOR SUE WITH JUST A YAWN!

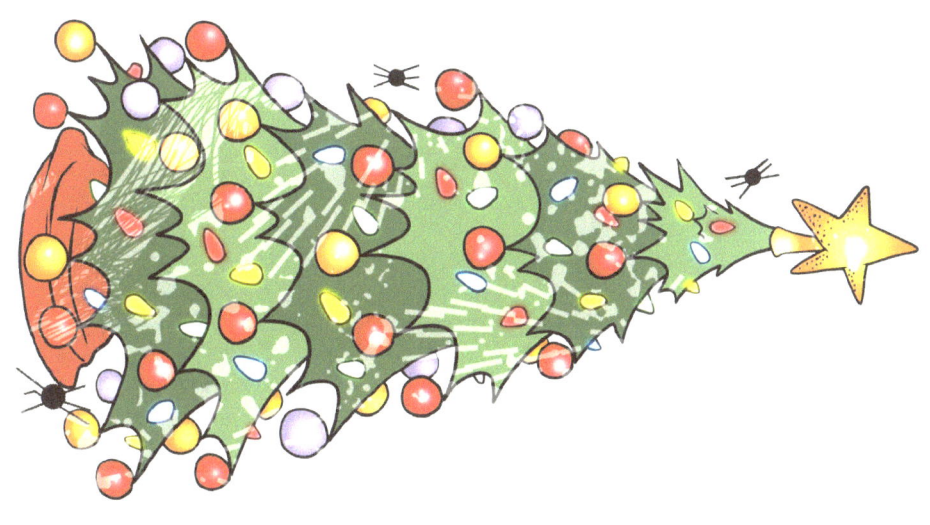

THEY PICKED THAT TREE UP BY THE STEM,

AND CARRIED IT AWAY WITH THEM!

WANT TO GUESS WHO CAME JUST AFTER?

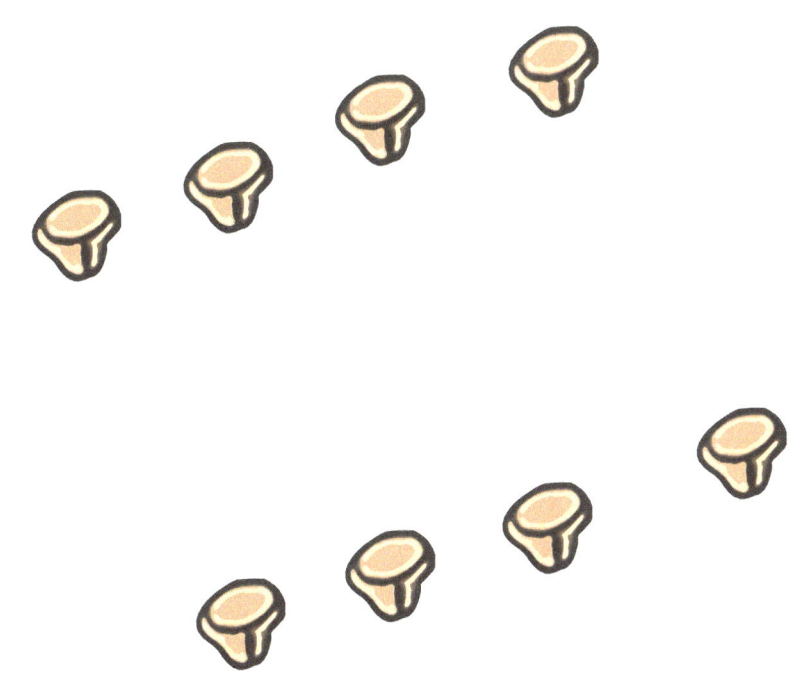

EIGHT SMALL REINDEER, FILLED WITH LAUGHTER!

THE RED-NOSED ONE SOON JOINED THE GAME,

'TIL SANTA'S VOICE LOUDLY PROCLAIMED:

ON DASHER, DANCER, AND THE REST!

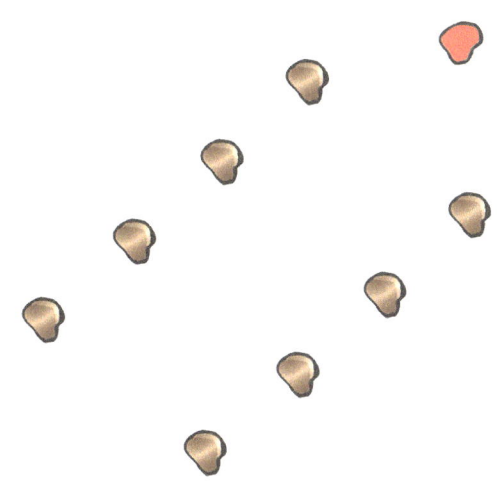

IT'S TIME TO MAKE THIS CHRISTMAS BEST!

i THOUGHT MY SHOW WAS OVER,
BUT...

THREE WHITE PENGUINS SAUNTERED UP!

THEY PLANTED CANDY CANES OUTSIDE,

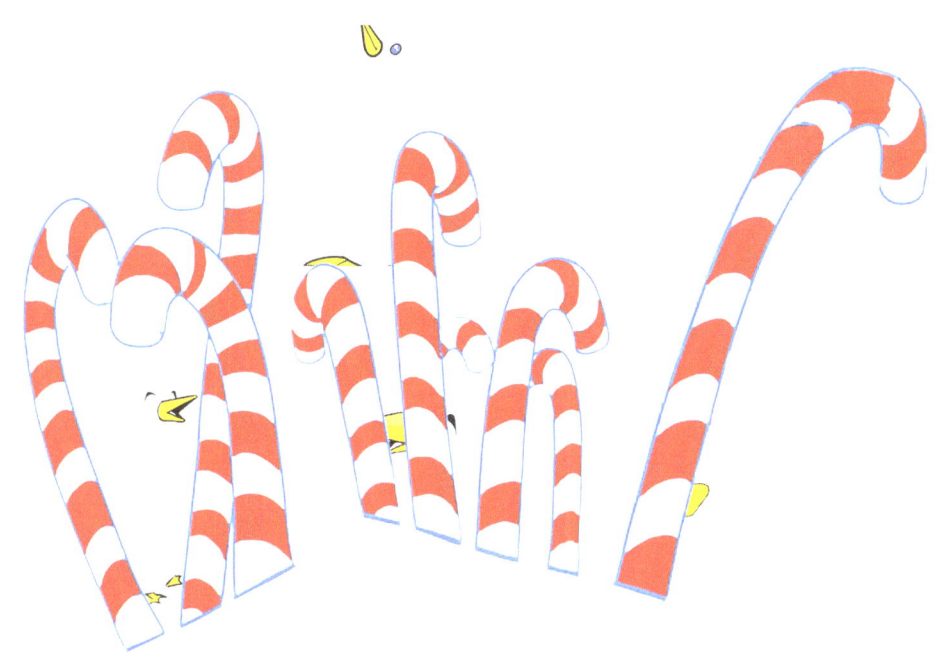

AND PLAYED A SPORT CALLED "SEEK-AND-HiDE!"

THE SNOW KEPT FALLING, DOWN, DOWN, DOWN...

WHEN CAME A SOUND FROM OVER-TOWN!

TEN WHITE GEESE HONK-HONKED RIGHT BY...

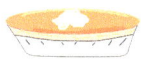

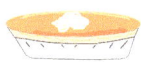

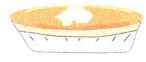
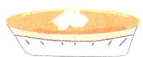

AND EACH ONE BROUGHT A PUMPKIN PIE!

IT MADE ME HUNGRY, THIS I'LL SAY,
I WANTED NO MORE SNOW THAT DAY.

WAIT.
WHAT DID I JUST HEAR FROM YOU?

YOU DON'T BELIEVE THIS TALE IS
TRUE?

WELL...

ASK THE BLIND MAN! HE SAW IT TOO!

www.ingramcontent.com/pod-product-compliance
Lightning Source LLC
Chambersburg PA
CBHW041815040426
42451CB00001B/6